# WHAT PEOPLE ARE SAYING ABOUT
## *CAN GOD DO IT?*

This is an amazing book. It strongly grabbed my attention—I thought I knew some of her stories, but I quickly realized I did not know the extent of them. This lady has always carried the Holy Spirit in her heart, and she talks with Him as if He is her friend.

—Bishop C. Horace Kitson

No wonder He gave her direction, protection, and encouragement, as well as four wonderful children.

So many ask, "Can God do this?" *Can God Do It?* settles the matter once and for all—not only can God do it, but He will do it again. Great job, sister Viviene! Continue to bring glory to the name of our Lord and Savior Jesus Christ.

—Dr. Lorna Kitson

*Can God Do It?* is a very encouraging and heart-stirring book. The transparency of personal accounts truly captivates the reader and pulls them into a familiar and relatable space. One can't help but be challenged by the convictions and commitment that are so real in each account. This book will inspire all who read it.

—Gareth Phillips

A life of faith, engaging the help and counsel of the Holy Spirit and complete dependence on the love and mercies of God the Father and His Son, Jesus Christ is what this life story is about. Mrs. Kitson has shared her fears and falls as well as her victories and successes in this "must read" documentary of a wife, mother, business woman and servant of God. I hope you will add this book to your library and let it encourage you to draw from the Holy Spirit to help you too in your life's journey.

—Vida Kitson

# CAN GOD DO IT?

A Journey of
Faith and Divine
Encounter

Viviene A. Kitson

K KUDU
PUBLISHING

ISBN: 978-1-962401-73-9     1 2 3 4 5 6 7 8 9 10

Printed in the United States of America

*In loving memory of my late husband, Derrick Kitson. Your unwavering support, selfless love, and constant encouragement have been my guiding light and steadfast anchor. Throughout our journey together, you were my confidant, my greatest supporter, and my source of inspiration. Your memory continues to motivate me every day.*

*I also dedicate this book to my four wonderful children: Simonie, Dean, Judyth, and David Kitson. Your unwavering belief in me, your endless patience, and your boundless love have been invaluable. Simonie, your wisdom and grace have been sources of strength; Dean, your resilience and determination have inspired me; Judyth, your creativity and kindness have uplifted me; and David, your humor, giftedness, and unwavering support have brightened my darkest days.*

*Thank you all for being my pillars of strength and for walking this path with me. This book is as much yours as it is mine.*

# CONTENTS

# ACKNOWLEDGMENTS

I would like to extend my deepest gratitude to everyone who has been instrumental in the creation of this manuscript. Your support, guidance, and encouragement have been invaluable throughout this journey.

Special thanks to those who provided spiritual guidance, insightful feedback, and unwavering support: Prophetess Dr. Amorelle Shemaiah, Gavin Hibbert, Giselle Johnny, and Lajoya Henriques. Your contributions, whether through wisdom, encouragement, or constructive criticism, have greatly enriched this work.

A heartfelt thank you to my beloved children: Simonie, Dean, Judyth, and David. Your unwavering support, patience, and love have been my pillars of strength and inspiration throughout this process.

I am also deeply grateful to John Åberg for his early editing efforts and to Safiya Brown and Leighton Forrest for their meticulous and thorough edits. Your editorial genius has contributed greatly to bringing this manuscript to its final form.

Special appreciation goes to my brother, Leonard Nicholson, for designing the cover of my book. Your creativity and artistic vision have beautifully captured the essence of this work.

To all of you, I extend my heartfelt thanks. This book would not have been possible without your support, encouragement, and contributions.

# INTRODUCTION

To properly understand this book and really appreciate the contents, you must first know that we are made up of spirit, soul, and body. The born-again experience, according to the Bible, is a spiritual relationship with the Godhead. The Holy Spirit is the third person of God.

Yes, that's right—He is a person.

A born-again experience with the Father, Son, and Holy Spirit gives you access to control and work in your life. You will hear me speak of the Holy Spirit often throughout this book. The Holy Spirit of God—our Friend, Confidant,

Teacher, and Counselor—reveals to us relationship, instructions, convictions, and persuasions.

In *The Release of the Spirit*, author Watchman Nee quotes, "God intended for man's spirit to be his home or dwelling place."[1] The Holy Spirit unites with the spirit of one who chooses Jesus Christ as Lord. That person then operates with divine help from the Deity, from God, in the form of the Holy Spirit. Our lives are to be lived from the spirit man, or "inner man," as Mr. Nee would explain. Our soul is the space that houses not just our emotions, but decisions and passions. The "inner man" is to rule this side of us. Mr. Nee refers to the soul as the "outer man." The body is the part of us with the least say in our lives. Mr. Nee explains the body as the expression of the unity of God's Spirit with our spirit, navigating and directing our passions, emotions, and decisions.

This is the story of my life. This is how I have had to learn to live.

---

1 Watchman Nee, *The Release of the Spirit* (Richmond, VA: Christian Fellowship Publishers, 2010), 2.

The Holy Spirit is the wisdom of God. Many times, we misrepresent Him and seek to draw attention to ourselves. We are to serve God and only God. Instead, we often accuse God of creating undesirable circumstances in our lives. We need to be careful about what we say when something doesn't work out the way we want it to. He longs for supernatural encounters with His people by working signs and wonders. He's a God of endless miracles.

The Holy Spirit has impacted my life in various ways. He has made me feel free to trust Him in everything I do. For years, He wanted me to know that surrendering to Him is easy. The Spirit knows what we need, so if you pay careful attention to Him, He will bless and help you make the right decisions. More than anything, He wants to live His life through us to the glory of the Father.

As you read, I want you to know that having the Holy Spirit as the center of your life makes all the difference. We feel His joy and strength in His manifested presence when we endure the turbulence of life.

But you must listen to Him and obey Him. It is God's will that you have a zealous relationship with the Holy Spirit that is contagious to everyone you come in contact with.

# CHAPTER 1

# IT NEARLY
# HAPPENED

They both came to an agreement that I should live with my father and my big sister live with my mother.

My mother told me that when my older sister was conceived, my grandfather was most disappointed with her for being pregnant. He showed my mother this when he pointed a pistol at my father on a day when he came to visit her. Two years later, I was conceived, and my father gave money to my mother to abort me. She took the money but was very confused and didn't know what to do. My many readers, if this selfish act had been done—and it nearly happened—the stories that you are about to read would not have taken place.

This is my story.

I was born in 1952 in Jamaica on a cool rainy September day. My mother was from Port Antonio, Portland, and my father was from Lucea, Hanover. I am the second child. Per their agreement, I stayed with my father, and he married another lady, Ms. Birdie. I grew up with them and Ms. Birdie's six biological children Harris, Leonard, Statesy, Joan, Carol, and Michelle from the age of two and was told that I would cry a lot while living with them. A Jamaican proverb says that little ones who cry a lot tend to be great singers. This proved to be true, as my father turned me loose on stages and outdoor events to sing. I was schooled up to the secondary level. I pursued both commercial and career studies, including international catering, and I also worked in the corporate world. I took Chinese courses to further my education and enhance and expand my portfolio.

My life has been quite a journey, and throughout this journey, I have learned to trust in my heavenly Father. I converted to Christianity when I was just fifteen years old. I got baptized and grew up in the church. My father and stepmother were Christians, so I always attended church (which I didn't mind at all, even before I became a Christian myself). Attending church with them, in part, made me who I am today.

**WE MADE EVERY EFFORT TO HAVE OUR OWN PERSONAL RELATIONSHIP WITH CHRIST, AND THROUGH THESE EFFORTS, WE GAINED GREATER CLARITY ON HOW TO LIVE AND CONDUCT OURSELVES AS CHRISTIANS.**

My life had many twists and turns. It has not been without its fair share of challenges, but with God's help, I've managed to pull through the many obstacles. Before my twenty-second birthday, I met my husband during a church fellowship. We began expressing our love for each other, and then our pastors told us that we had to be married within three months, so we had a short engagement period. We got married in December 1974. On our wedding night, I felt timid and pondered my husband and I expressing our love for each other as we awkwardly lay side-by-side. Considering this would be my first experience with a man in bed, for a moment, I wanted to go back home.

**Our Wedding Day**

Our marriage got interesting. We started with a few hours of morning devotion, especially on Saturday mornings, which has added much to our lives throughout the years. Between studying the Word and preparing for church, we learned to study each other. We were devoted to God and each other, and we were together for forty-two years.

We were blessed with four children, two boys and two girls. Our lives had their challenges, and we learned from them. We learned how to walk together, pray together, read the Scriptures together, worship together, cry together, and just be there for each other, hand in hand, arm in arm. We understood what it meant to submit to each other, but it wasn't without rough spots and breaks in communication along the way. The commitment we made to remain together matured us in Christ and His Word. Yes, there were times when we bent and broke down beneath the weight of marriage, but not for long, as the Holy Spirit spoke and showed us how to bounce back from our blunders. We made every effort to have our own personal relationship with Christ, and through these efforts, we gained greater clarity on how to live and conduct ourselves as Christians. We had corporate devotions before and after having children, as we knew this was essential to keeping us and our family on the right path towards purpose and destiny. Remaining steadfast and consistent in our efforts was a mainstay in our lives, as we both came from pastors' homes. We remained convicted to carry out our fathers' examples.

## BUILDING A FAMILY

Our first home was just off Molynes Road, Kingston, Jamaica, where our first child was born. We spent a lot of time getting to know each other, reading Scripture, praying together, and allowing God to become evident in our lives. During this time when finances were a bit tight, I got to know the Lord and what He expected of me as a young woman. It was challenging to simultaneously raise a child and serve the Lord. Our first three children were close in age, so at that time, I didn't work for approximately five and a half years and had to learn how to trust the Lord to provide whatever we needed. I wanted to work, but finding employment was difficult. I discerned that the Holy Spirit was leading me to spend time training up our children because people would come to me for help and advice on how to train up their children.

We were firmly established in kingdom work in both our family and spiritual lives, but being home with the children was trying

Young Kitsons

because, above all, their needs had to be met. We had to live by faith, as the scripture says, "The just shall live by faith" (Romans 1:17). My husband was a very good provider for the family, even though there were tough times. He felt the weight and pain of it. He was a certified teacher for the government and a skilled tailor who sought to bring in additional income for the family. We were both evangelists in our church, so we had to balance church duties with our duties to each other and as parents to our children.

I am very grateful for how good the Lord has been to us. He has given us so much strength to pull through our most difficult times together. Before I left my parents' home, I was very fearful of taking big steps and striving towards greater things. I was raised in an environment of fear. The fear did not come from my parents but from the false perception that in order to excel in life, I needed more academic qualifications. Despite that, I still tried and forged my path into the marketplace. Because of my commitment and surrender to Jesus Christ for strength, I have managed to overcome that fear.

> **BECAUSE OF MY COMMITMENT AND SURRENDER TO JESUS CHRIST FOR STRENGTH, I HAVE MANAGED TO OVERCOME THAT FEAR.**

The key takeaway is that complete dependence on God can literally change the trajectory of your life. I have learned to have an intimate relationship with Him. His Son and the Holy Spirit gave me the courage to take on the shadows of life, boldly and shamelessly.

# CHAPTER 2

# A SIGN AFTER BIRTH

*"And all thy children* **shall be** *taught of the L*ORD*;*
*and great* **shall be** *the peace of thy children."*

—Isaiah 54:13

Our first daughter was born at home. When I was ready to have my child, we did not know what gender the child would be. My mother-in-law was there, and the nurse from the hospital came to our home. The labor pains were sharp, and the delivery was very quick. After delivery, the nurse took the baby, wrapped her, and placed her on her side to drain the mucus from her mouth. We heard the nurse cry out and say, "Oh, the baby is praying!" To my amazement, I saw my daughter on her knees in a praying position with her little buttocks in the air. I then understood the significance of that moment.

At the time, my husband was terrified of holding a baby, but the fear didn't stop him from the joy of holding his daughter.

After the nurse cleaned her up, my daughter was placed on her side in a cot by my bed, and once again, she reverted to the praying position she was in before—on her knees. We were all still amazed at what we were seeing—understanding it as a sign of our prayer and commitment to the Lord. So, we knew that our daughter—our eldest—would become an intercessor. Today, she moves heavily in the prophetic and intercessory anointing and is also a qualified teacher.

The next day, my husband went to work. Upon returning home in the afternoon, he greeted me and his daughter and then told me that the Lord had given him a word from Isaiah 54:13, "And all thy children *shall be* taught of the LORD: and great *shall be* the peace of thy children." When he read that verse, my response was, "Does it mean that we are going to have more children?" Having just felt the pain of childbirth, I was not sure I wanted to go through it again. Yet, the Holy Spirit revealed to me that this scripture covered our four children. And just under the age of thirty, we had our quiver full—four children were born to us.

## WHEN PLANS CHANGE

We were planning on moving from where we were living at the time. Before we left, I thought I was pregnant again, and I worried it was too soon to have another child. One morning, our prayer partner came to the house and asked if everything was okay. I told him my concerns about the possibility of being pregnant again. He and I prayed together.

He prayed, "Lord, give your daughter a word." Shortly after he left, the Lord spoke to me from 1 Corinthians 4:5:

*"Therefore judge nothing before the time, until the Lord come, who both will bring to light the hidden things of darkness, and will make manifest the counsels of the hearts: and then shall every man have praise of God."*

IT BECAME A PRACTICE FOR ME AND MY HUSBAND TO HEAR WHAT GOD WAS SAYING IN HIS WORD BEFORE WE MADE ANY STEP OR DECISION AT ALL.

After I read the Word, I felt like I needed to use the bathroom. Once I got there, to my surprise, my menstrual cycle began. My anxiety and concern were eradicated, and I was filled with peace. Hallelujah! I have learned from that experience that the Lord will help and see me through whatever I need from Him. It became a practice for me and my husband to hear what God was saying in His Word before we made any step or decision at all.

We were ready when our first son was born and filled with glee—now, we had a pair! The slogan in our country at that time was, "Two is better than too many." My husband was very happy and suggested we stop at two, and I agreed. Today, my first-born son and his wife are the owners of a successful business. They are heavily involved in music, and he plays the drums at his church. They also have four children of their own.

Then, a surprise showed up at our doorstep! Only two years later, I was pregnant with my third child. This conception terrified my husband! I was not sure what to feel or do, so I came into agreement with him. We asked the Lord to take this child. I remember it so clearly—as if it were yesterday. We were neither mentally nor physically prepared for this pregnancy. As my husband and I did our regular morning devotions, we sat on our bed, looked at each other, and thought, *How are we going to get through this one?* My husband said that we would have to ask the Lord to take it. He said he did not have the finances and time to give to three children. We prayed and believed for God to abort this pregnancy, but nothing happened.

We were accustomed to asking the Lord for a word in every situation, so we settled down and humbled ourselves and asked the Lord for a word regarding our unborn child. We prayed and waited in His presence for a while. Then, a word came to my husband's spirit, "For God hath caused me to be fruitful in the land of my affliction" (Genesis 41:52).

We were confident about the word the Spirit of the Lord gave us; we resolved in our hearts that God would work this out for our good—and hers. The prophetic word went before her in such a way that the scripture itself was fulfilled. Our daughter has been able to prosper and be fruitful in the land of her affliction. Presently, this child, who is a psychologist and worship leader, lives in Europe with her husband who is a professor and teacher. Her affliction manifested itself through extreme circumstances that her husband and she have had to bear with their family, but we are immensely grateful for the times we are able to spend with her family, which includes our three grandchildren.

So this word was prophetic, and the Angel of the Lord could work on the word while she was in a strange land— Europe—bringing to pass what was decreed over her as a baby, a child and a young woman.

We were in for one final surprise—I had now conceived our fourth child. We were not in a good place this time around, especially my husband. He was not communicating well with me and blamed me for it. His words cut deep and were highly offensive. Instead of bringing it to me directly, he handed me a letter that said he was through, and it was not his fault. I was shocked. I realized that I had no other option but to make it a matter of prayer. So, that's what I did. I brought it all to Him and immersed myself in the Word of God.

Communication with my husband was strained, but we tried anyway. One day, as the time of delivery was drawing near, he took me to my appointment at the clinic, even though he said he wouldn't. He always carried around a very small pocket Bible with him to pray. While I was with my doctor, the Holy Spirit instructed him to open up his Bible and read Psalm 115:3, "But our God is in the heavens: He hath done whatsoever he hath pleased," and 12-14:

> The LORD hath been mindful of us: he will bless us; He will bless the house of Israel; He will bless the house of Aaron. He will bless them that fear the LORD, both small and great. The LORD shall increase you more and more, you and your children.

The Holy Spirit also told my husband to name our son David. Today, both David and his wife are teachers. He is a program coordinator for elderly citizens, a family man, and a pastor of his own congregation in New York.

The Lord was birthing new things, and we knew there was much more to come.

# CHAPTER 3

# A LIFE OF FAITH AND BREAKTHROUGHS

While we were worshiping at the Maxfield Chapel at the Ritz Theatre, I felt the urge to walk around Maxfield Avenue in Kingston to see if I could find a job in that area. I wanted to continue seeking God on what He willed, so I could contribute to my family's finances. One morning, I crossed the road from the church as the Spirit of the Lord led me and encountered a businessman who was the sole proprietor of the famous Bird Cage Restaurant located in the downtown area. He asked me, "What do you do for a living?" I told him I was a caterer, and he suggested that I visit his restaurant. This restaurant was established many years ago and has an excellent reputation. I had the opportunity to meet him and his sister, and I was offered a job on the spot as a supervisor. I observed their catering style and other services, which was exciting for me. So, I continued there for a little while.

On my way to work, I would usually read Scripture on the bus from home to downtown Kingston. One morning, while traveling on the bus, the Spirit of the Lord prompted me to look up. When I did, I saw a Best Dressed Chicken advertisement street sign. The Holy Spirit said to me, *You can be a wholesaler that sells chickens.* I responded in my spirit, *Really, Lord?* and visualized obtaining chicken from a farmer or distributor to sell wholesale. The Spirit of the Lord said to me that I could do this to help myself and the family. The idea never left me, and each time I drove, I felt a burden in my heart that I could begin a wholesale business. I remember the thought that came to me—*Just a*

*Sign*—which would have been the title of that testimony. Because it was "just a sign," I did not say anything to my husband yet; instead, I meditated on it and sought the Lord's direction.

Within that year, I spoke to one of our church sisters who lived in Portmore. She visited us one morning, and I asked her, "Do you know of anywhere that I could set up a wholesale?"

She informed me, "Sister Kitson, there is a wholesale store not far from my business place, but they are not getting a lot of sales. Sometimes, they are open, and then the next day, they are closed." She offered to check it out and get back to me.

When she returned, she informed me, "Sister Kitson, this wholesale is closing down for good, so I am going to see if I can find the person who oversees the property so that, by faith, you could get it."

So, she began her search and returned with great news. My husband and I went to the owner of a big property called the Portmore Entertainment Center. The wholesale was right at the front, and I felt in my heart that this was the right location for our business. Derrick and I got in touch with the owner, and negotiations began. We also contacted the individuals who operated the wholesale before us and acquired some of their equipment with their permission, as we rented the wholesale from the owner.

We set out by faith, and the Lord helped us stock the place. We also went to two places where we could get goods on hire purchase because we did not have the money to purchase all the goods at one time. As we were preparing to get our business up and running, my mother, who was living in the US, passed away, and her body was brought down to Jamaica to be buried. This delayed our launch. It was during this time that I obtained my US visa. Since I did not have the opportunity to visit her while she was sick, I went to visit my siblings in September. I spent about two weeks in the United States along with my sister. My mother left funds for her five children. I received my portion and bought quite a few things to bring back home for my family and the church.

On my flight home, the Holy Spirit said to me, *You have not given Me my portion*, referring to a love offering. So, I asked the Holy Spirit, "How much do You want me to give towards Your work?" and He said to me, "$5,000." I wholeheartedly obliged. I was very grateful that my mom left money for us, so I pledged to give that sum towards the Lord's work.

> **WE HAD NEVER EXPERIENCED A VACATION LIKE THAT BEFORE AS A FAMILY, AND WE SAW THE GOODNESS OF GOD IN THE LAND OF THE LIVING.**

When I returned home, I had enough money to pay rent and buy a few more goods for wholesale. With this, we approached two business places to see if we could get goods on hire purchase to stock the wholesale. We succeeded with a company called Industrial Sales—our first main source of assistance. When we arrived, we knew the Lord was allowing us to pursue it. We spoke with the purchasing manager in late November of 1996. He initially declined because the peak of December was too busy. However, after some conversation, he relented and provided us with approximately $36,000 worth of goods. We were grateful and started with that. We then approached another business organization, and with an introduction from a friend who had a business, we received another $15,000 worth of goods.

With these acquisitions, including some minor goods, we still lacked some important goods in our large wholesale and felt embarrassed. However, we remained grateful and focused on stocking the shelves and reflecting on what God *had* provided.

We were able to open the business on December 15, 1996. We named it Kits Wholesale, and God, by His great might and wisdom, helped us. Within a year, we made a million dollars, which was incredible. In the second year, we took our entire family of six on vacation somewhere along the North Coast. We had never experienced that before as a family, and we saw the goodness of God in the land of the living. It was an awesome experience.

During this period, despite the blessings of the Lord, we experienced gunmen in the marketplace, at our home, and our business on three different occasions, but the Lord was with us and delivered us.

> *"They that trust in the* LORD *shall be as mount Zion, which cannot be removed, but abideth forever. As the mountains are round about Jerusalem, so the* LORD *is round about his people from henceforth even forever."—Psalm 125:1-2*

## HOME PROTECTION

Yes, this life was real. We were seeing and living it. The Lord had given us victory. At our home one day, two gunmen climbed our property wall and came to the back of the house while my husband and I were on the verandah with a business employee discussing the closing of our restaurant business. We had a bag of cash that rested by the front door. Both of our sons were home—one child was at the dining table and another in the bedroom. By the glory of God, they were not harmed.

My son sounded the alarm that we were in danger when he said that someone was here to see us. We knew this was fishy, so my husband ran to get help. Our employee commanded the gunman not to shoot, so my husband was spared. The bag of money was supernaturally invisible to the gunman— his foot even brushed it! Both gunmen left through the back door, climbed over the wall, and released shots into the night sky. The Lord divinely protected us from all harm. Can GOD do it? Yes! He can.

Psalm 91:11 says, "For he shall give his angels charge over thee, to keep thee in all thy ways." This was what we knew. This is what we still know and believe as a family.

## WHOLESALE BUSINESS PROTECTION

Along with our staff, we began each morning and ended each night with prayer. Our eldest son, Dean, worked with us full-time, and the other children worked on weekends. Today, he and his family have a thriving business of their own and follow the same spiritual practice of opening and closing in prayer.

So, God honored us by prospering the wholesale. We were very grateful; we had a staff of about five people, plus our own children. It was just amazing! We saw firsthand how God loves and cares for His own. Every breakthrough came from a prayerful life with family and fellowship of the saints. It came out of our giving ourselves selflessly to God and caring for others.

My husband and I would leave our business in capable hands and sacrifice a day or two each week for fasting and prayer in the house of God. It was quite a season for us—and also an adventure—just to see how God cares for His own. He is our provider.

As we were closing one late Christmas Eve night, my husband came out with our son and with bags of money in hand, a young man held him up with a short chrome pistol pushed against my husband's back. The young man said to him, "Give me all you have," and my husband responded out loud, "The blood of Jesus Christ is against you!" The young man staggered, and the gun fell from his hand. My husband was about to take it up, and the young man grabbed it and ran into the community while declaring in Jamaican dialect, "Is wah dis mi go do? Is wah dis mi go do?" In English, this means, "Why did I do this? Why did I do this?"

> **GOD HAS WORKED ON OUR BEHALF, AND WE CONTINUE TO WHOLEHEARTEDLY BELIEVE IN HIM.**

My husband's rebuke was the talk of the town that evening. We heard the chatter and cautiously came out of our house.

Others came out of their homes and entered the wholesale because they heard the loud rebuking of the Lord and wanted to know what was happening. Once God made clear to the people what was going on, they shouted, "But he is crazy! He can't hold up the pastor's business place!" God showed up for us miraculously. The gunman took nothing from us, and none of us was hurt. We say, "To God be the glory!" It was and still is an interesting milestone and journey for us, while we had business over in Newlands, Portmore. God has worked on our behalf, and we continue to wholeheartedly believe in Him.

# CHAPTER 4

# THE POWER OF PRAYER

After the birth of our first child, we received a verbal warning from our landlord that we were not to participate in evangelistic work. We had been praying for a sick neighbor in our home, and when she came to us for prayer, she entered through the protective gate onto our landlord's property. We suspected that she was one of those who used profane language, and the landlord was displeased with her conduct. He said to us, "Leave my house and do your mission elsewhere because my house is not a mission field!" We asked the Lord to deal with the situation for us, as we were only doing what he commanded: "Go ye into all the world, and preach the gospel to every creature" (Mark 16:15). A short time after, he gave us a formal notice and disrespected my husband a few times. My husband, empowered by the Holy Spirit, said, "The Lord rebuke you! Hold your peace!" The landlord replied, "I will hold my peace." And he never said another word to us until we left some months later.

Before we left for the new location, we brought the notice before the Lord and knelt by our bedside, asking God to work for us, as we needed a more conducive environment to do God's work. The Lord spoke and showed me a house next door to my father's house. At the time, I did not want to go to that area because my father was very strict, and I just did not want to be anywhere near that attitude. Even so, we went to check out the house God showed me. Someone lived there, but I proceeded with a fearful knock at the gate. A gentleman approached us as we asked about the house being up for rent. He told us that while he was

still occupying the house, he would be moving soon. We
needed somewhere to live as soon as possible, but he told
us he would need longer than one month. So, we rented
another place on the same avenue.

After a few months, we checked back with the man living
at the house next to my father. It was vacant. The owners
asked us about our budget. The Lord, by His Holy Spirit,
had previously shown me that I was to pay JMD$80 for
rent. I hesitated because I feared that was too low. I didn't
want to seem presumptuous, especially in a situation like
this. The lady asked if we could pay JMD$90. My husband
and I glanced at each other and agreed to the amount.
Little did we know that the previous tenant was paying
JMD$70. We had disobeyed. Even though our rent was
higher than we preferred, we lived there for approximately
thirteen years, paying less than JMD$100, and our rent
was never increased once. I'll ask you again: Can GOD
do it?

> ## MY FAITH IN HIS PROVISION ALLOWED OUR RELATIONSHIP TO CONTINUOUSLY GROW.

God was indeed good to us over the years. He has shown himself as our provider many times. He is *Jehovah-Jireh*, which means the Lord will provide (Genesis 22:14). My faith in His provision allowed our relationship to continuously grow. When the house was up for sale, the realtors gave my husband and me first priority as potential buyers. The house went for about JMD$139,000, but my husband was convinced we would not need to pay that amount. So, he made an offer at half price. Buyers came to look at the home, but we walked around the house and claimed the property as our own. We prayed much and solicited prayer from the church. The owner of the house grew sick and passed away. Although we didn't get the house for exactly half the selling price, we still got the house for much less, at JMD$86,000!

In addition, we were able to build onto the house and pay off all our expenses. Our lives have been a journey of faith and breakthroughs. We always shared what we believed the Lord was speaking to us and involved our children in family decisions so that they could have their own relationship with Christ and partake of the same favor and blessing we experienced.

> *"If ye be willing and obedient, ye shall eat the good of the land: But if ye refuse and rebel, ye shall be devoured with the sword: for the mouth of the Lord hath spoken it."—Isaiah 1:19-20*

## FIRST ANNIVERSARY FAITH TRIP

In early August of 1984, I was working at a large corporation when the Holy Spirit spoke to my heart about my anniversary. I was moved to ask a male friend of mine if he knew of anywhere on the North Coast where my husband and I could spend a weekend for our anniversary in December. Sometime later, he found a place but admitted it would be a little expensive. I felt it was the Holy Spirit that laid this on my heart, so I began to think and pray. I spoke with the owner of the resort about my interest in reserving a room to celebrate our tenth anniversary. She did not have a one-bedroom apartment but offered her own little room! I was a bit disappointed but still happy that my husband and I would get the chance to be alone together for the first time since having children. She told me that she would let us stay there for a cost of JMD$400. A few days before we made the final arrangement, she warned us that the room was small and dusty because she stays there only when she comes from Kingston to rent and do business. I told her we were very grateful and would still accept it.

## SHE THEN HANDED US AN ENVELOPE WITH THE KEY AND TOLD US THAT HER BOSS HAD CHANGED HER MIND.

The day came for us to travel to the North Coast for our

Our Anniversary

anniversary vacation. On our way to the cottage, my husband and I chatted, and I laughed about how we would be spending time alone without our four children. When we arrived, the receptionist asked us our names and confirmed our stay at the lady's cottage. She then handed us an envelope with the key and told us that her boss had changed her mind. Instead, she offered a two-bedroom apartment for an additional cost of only JMD$80! We were very shocked, surprised, and a bit speechless to see how God had exceeded our expectations.

Can GOD do it? Yes! He can.

The two-bedroom apartment was large and had all the necessary facilities—and at such a small cost! We kept thinking about God's wonderful deed. We gave thanks to God for making it possible and enjoyed the spacious place He provided us.

We prayed, ate, laughed, and made future plans concerning our children and church family. God is good!

# CHAPTER 5

# WHEN GOD'S SPIRIT SPEAKS

C an GOD do it? One morning, in the early part of 2021, I was cleaning up my bedroom when the Spirit of the Lord spoke to my heart and told me that they had cut the bunch of bananas hanging over my neighbor's fence. Immediately, I went to investigate and saw the banana tree extended across the neighbor's property. To my surprise (though I shouldn't have been surprised—it came from the Holy Spirit, after all!), the Spirit of the Lord clearly spoke

John 10:27, "My sheep hear my voice, and I know them, and they follow me." My neighbor and his friends had their jerk pan and a big pot ready for cooking right next to my fence, so I asked my neighbor's friends to call him for me. When he came to the fence, I requested that he give me the bananas that were cut. I took the bunch from him. Because I was confident that the Spirit of the Lord had spoken, I did not even ask him if he had cut the bananas. The experience was tremendous. Proverbs 3:5-6 instructs us to:

> *"Trust in the* LORD *with all thine heart; and lean not unto thine own understanding. In all thy ways acknowledge him, and he shall direct thy paths."*

## SALVATION FOR ELDERLY MEN

During our tenure at Waltham Park Road church, I responded to the deep calling on my life from a young age and worked in evangelism. Even as a teenager, I would talk to someone on the bus about the Lord Jesus Christ and on the carport at my home, teaching Sunday school. I felt the urge to reach the lost. While supporting my husband in pastoral ministry, we made regular visits to the church community. We were informed of an elderly man experiencing health challenges, so our regular visits led us to his home on several occasions for prayer and healing. Eventually, he was restored, invited Jesus into his life, and began to attend church services. Some months later, he departed for his heavenly home to be with his Lord.

The Holy Spirit frequently prompted me to conduct street meetings in our community. One elderly mother in our church was zealous for the salvation of her husband. Led by the Holy Spirit, I regularly visited with one or two others in their home and shared a word with her husband. He would always smile and agree with what I said and appeared interested in living a different lifestyle. Unfortunately, there was no movement towards salvation.

We planned evangelism outreach, and he attended the meetings. Eventually, he was ready to invite Jesus into his heart. He was baptized, and we were all thankful for his deliverance from sin. Shortly after his conversion, he left for his heavenly home in 1993 to be with his Savior and Lord.

I continued to reach out to the elderly community. Dudley was one of my favorites in the community where I attended church. I made every effort to visit him regularly, especially when I attended services. On several Monday evenings, I would slip out of service to visit with and witness to him. His wife, a member of our congregation who sang in the choir at the time, also desired her husband's salvation. One evening, despite his promises to come to church, he did not show up for service. So, I went to visit him. Instead of just checking in on him and leaving, I decided to wait. As the time approached 9:00 pm, Dudley realized I was serious about waiting for him. Eventually, he got ready, and we went to the house of God together. He left the church during prayer.

On my next visit, he mentioned that when he had left the church that night, he nearly died falling into a ditch. This incident seemed to affect him, and he became less resistant to my visits. Later, in January, I reluctantly shared with him a dream I had that he was dying. In March of the same year, he confessed Jesus as his Lord and Savior and received water baptism.

My visits with Dudley continued, and I must admit that after a while, I forgot about the dream. I shared scriptures with him and kept up with visitations. Days and months passed. Around December 20, my husband and I arrived at the church gate for youth service, and someone informed us that Dudley had passed away. I was frightened, curious, and anxious to see him at his home where he was sitting up in a chair motionless and covered with a white sheet. I did not remember the dream. However, after some time with his family and our church family, the Holy Spirit reminded me of it. I was shocked that what the Holy Spirit had revealed to me came true. Second Peter 3:9 reassures us that "The Lord is not slack concerning his promise, as some men count slackness; but is longsuffering to us-ward, not willing that any should perish, but that all should come to repentance."

## A NEW CHAPTER

In February of 1983, the Holy Spirit spoke to my husband while serving in ministry with his father to serve in three different assemblies.

The Lord spoke to him, as He did Abraham:

> *Get thee out of thy country, from thy kindred,*
> *and from thy father's house, unto a land that I will*
> *show thee; And I will make of thee a great nation,*
> *and I will bless thee, and make thy name great; and*
> *thou shalt be a blessing: And I will bless them that*
> *bless thee; and curse him that curseth thee: and*
> *in thee shall all families of the earth be blessed.*
> *—Genesis 12:1-3*

We felt the leading of the Spirit of God transition us into our calling.

In July 2003, the Lord told my husband to meet with Him in prayer and fasting to receive direction concerning ministry. The Holy Spirit gave him the scripture, "For a great door and effectual is opened unto me, and there are many adversaries" (1 Corinthians 16:9). A few days later, a bishop and prophet from Trinidad and Tobago stayed at our home. Before leaving, he prayed with us, and the Lord spoke through him, calling my husband "Bishop" and repeating the same scripture He had given him. We received this confirmation from the Lord.

My husband had just completed thirty-four years of teaching with the Ministry of Education in Jamaica. We left for Orlando, Florida, and met with my husband's younger brother and his family to seek the Lord in prayer and fasting. In Florida, we stayed with an elderly church sister named Silda and her husband from Cleveland, Ohio, who invited us to spend a few weeks with them.

> **THE HOLY SPIRIT HAD COMPLETED A WORK IN HIS HEART THROUGH THE PRAYERS OF HIS WIFE AND OTHERS.**

We spent time between Florida and Ohio, following the Holy Spirit's instruction. In late September, we settled into our friend's home on a Thursday afternoon and enjoyed the new environment. The climate was colder as winter approached. Later that Thursday evening, our sister asked us to pray with them throughout the weekend. Our sister's husband and I prepared breakfast in the kitchen on Sunday morning. He and I began singing together, and then he shared that he had returned to the Lord and felt overwhelmed with joy. It had been approximately twenty years since he had stepped away from his commitment to God. The Holy Spirit had completed a work in his heart through the prayers of his wife and others, culminating in our visit. Two Sundays later, he was baptized, and we maintained communication with him.

About five years later, he passed away, and I was privileged to attend his funeral service. The Word of God declares in 1 Corinthians 3:6, "I have planted, Apollos watered; but God gave the increase." Approximately five years after his passing, his wife also went home to be with the Lord. We were grateful for the invitation to their home and the time spent together.

## EVERY NO IS A YES!

On one Friday around 1995, the Lord spoke to my heart by His Holy Spirit. I had been complaining to Him about my greatest need: ending the days of living hand to mouth. I needed a change. The Lord then told me to go to Banbury House of Prayer and Praise Ministries in Banbury, Linstead. This house had a fasting service. I agreed, unsure of how I was going to get there. At that exact time, the Holy Spirit said to me, *Call Vida.* Vida is my husband's sister, so I called her and shared what the Holy Spirit had instructed me to do. She also felt the Holy Spirit prompting her to attend, and responding with such exuberance, she agreed to drive. She was so excited that she even took time off of work to attend!

In Wednesday's fasting service, the moderator asked me what I wanted from the Lord. I shared that I needed God to provide a stable job so that I wouldn't have to eat from hand to mouth anymore. I wanted to sufficiently provide for my family. Those in attendance heard my heart's request.

The moderator invited us to the altar. It was there that I poured out my soul in prayer to the Lord, voicing my request. On our return to Kingston, I was very hopeful as my friend and I discussed the service and believed that something supernatural had happened. On Thursday morning, after my personal devotional time, I rose to my knees and went back to bed to lie in my husband's arms. The Holy Spirit quietly showed me a building on Red Hills Road in Kingston and spoke to me, *You can get this place for rent.* In the quietness of my thoughts, I said, *I don't have any money to rent a place.* Here He was, opening a door for me, and I was fearful. To be honest, I did not share it with my husband because I believed he would disagree, so I held it closely.

Rising from my husband's arms, the whisper of the Holy Spirit said to me, *Fast.* I quickly agreed as I got dressed to make breakfast. I was unsure of how things would go from here. I cooked lunch for children of a school nearby to purchase for JMD$10. This was certainly not enough to meet my needs, but using my skills was somewhat fulfilling.

That same morning, two young people from the congregation where we served visited. The Holy Spirit spoke to me and said, *Go and look at the place.* I knew the location He was referencing. By this time, my husband had already left for work. I asked the young visitors to help me serve the children as they came to purchase lunch, instructed them on what to do, and then got in the shower, where I heard the voice of the Holy Spirit say, *Claim it!*

My hands began moving up and down as I shouted, "I claim it!" about six times or more. This was my first experience with such timely instructions.

Fear started to creep in when I left for the location that I saw in the vision. I pushed past the fears and asked someone at the front desk if they had anywhere to rent. They directed me to a gate, but I passed it. Then and there, the Holy Spirit said to me, *Turn back and knock.* I still felt nervous but continued to push past it. Many have cited the acronym for fear: False. Evidence. Appearing. Real.

> **GOD GAVE ME THE COURAGE TO TELL HIM WHAT HE, BY HIS SPIRIT, SHOWED AND TOLD ME ABOUT THE PLACE.**

Knocking at the gate, a young man came to greet me. I asked if they had a place available to rent. He replied, "My uncle is not here. He is off the island. You'll have to come back at a later date." As I reached for my pen and paper to take his number, his uncle appeared at the gate! We looked at him with surprise. He took over the conversation and told me straight up that he had nowhere to rent.

I stood there, knowing in my heart that the Spirit of God had shown me this place. The uncle asked me what I was looking for. I told him I would like to sell some snacks like buns and cheese, along with other things. Again, he maintained and repeated many times that he did not have a place to rent out to me. He also continued to ask me about the space that I needed. Finally, he said that there were two shops upstairs, but nobody would want to go upstairs to buy food.

God gave me the courage to tell him what He, by His Spirit, had shown and told me about the place. He was confused and kept asking me what I wanted to do. I responded like before, "To sell snacks."

The gentleman said, with an outburst, "Do you want to cook?"

I stuttered in amazement and said, "If there is an available facility."

Sounding frightened, he said, "Follow me!" I followed behind him. With enthusiasm, he swung open a door and exclaimed, "This can help you!" It was a huge kitchen packed with furniture from a carpentry business.

Now I was feeling a bit frightened and surprised. I said, "Yes, sir."

Directly across from this kitchen, I followed him to his office, and he hastily asked me, "How much can you pay for rent? How much can you pay for rent?" I thought of an amount but didn't want to say it. He shouted, "I can't do business like this!" He was either nervous or very afraid. I'm not sure how the Holy Spirit dealt with him. He gave me his number and told me to call and return in two weeks' time.

I went home feeling hopeful. When my husband came home, I began relating the story to him. Two weeks had passed, and we both went to see the landlord. He said to my husband, "I told your wife I have nowhere to rent!" We continued talking, and he said, "Let me give you a tour of the place." It was a big complex. Upstairs and downstairs. He then told us he could have the two spaces ready for us within a few weeks. (He was offering the prime areas that would be good for my business—downstairs and not upstairs.) He said, "You can pay me the rent when you begin the business." There was no down payment required. The rent wasn't too expensive—JMD$600. He then remarked, "I am giving Mrs. Kitson two years to set herself up."

We were very grateful. We were able to start delivering lunches, from two to one hundred per day. It was a booming business, and I loved it. The Lord provided me with a business in my career of choice. This was a good start for us. Can GOD do it? Yes! He can.

# CHAPTER 6

# WHEN FAITH
# WALKS ON WATER

I traveled from Jamaica to Hong Kong to the United States for surgery. I had what is called a prolapsed bladder, which affects the urinary passage. The hospital in my hometown only offered a C-section surgery. At that time, I could not see myself undergoing another C-section. I was given a ring measuring 5 cm to insert to prevent the usual descent of the bladder; this lasted for two years, and it helped somewhat, but I could no longer live my life in that discomfort.

A friend of mine had undergone the same surgery that I needed overseas. It didn't come without challenges, but God worked it out for her. I prayed that the Lord would lead me in this area.

My friends told me that I would have to be in the country for some time to see what could be done. Of course, it was not possible; my husband had suffered a major accident in June 2014, falling from a fruit tree in the back of our home. Prior to this, there were building blocks around the fruit tree. One day, the Holy Spirit spoke to my husband about removing the blocks from around the tree root. Most of them were removed, leaving about three broken pieces buried halfway in the earth. The day my husband fell about twelve feet high from the tree, his head was near one of the pieces of the block when he fell. I believe if he had not heeded the Holy Spirit's instruction to remove the blocks, he could have lost his life. As I was taking a shower, he called out to me twice. I was frightened when he told me that he had fallen. I did not know what to do, so I panicked, circling the room and the hallway. Even in that state, my lover, my provider, my protector settled me with his voice.

He called my name and said to me, "Everything is going to be alright." Like a mother comforts a wailing child, I immediately felt calm.

> ## GOD HAD MIRACULOUSLY HEALED THE BROKEN BONES IN HIS BACK.

I returned to my senses and immediately made a call to my son and my husband's brother. We rushed him to the hospital. The X-ray showed he had broken three bones in his lower back. His right knee was also broken. He was admitted to the hospital Thursday afternoon. On Saturday morning, while visiting with him, the doctor sat him up and asked him if he was feeling any pain in his back. My husband said he did not! My son and I were amazed at this. God had miraculously healed the broken bones in his back. The doctor discharged him after putting a cast on his knee.

My husband's broken back was healed within two days. They set a date for knee surgery, but God had other plans. Instead, I took him to his physical therapist twice a week. Shortly after, while my husband was still recuperating, my daughter asked me to fly out to Hong Kong to assist her in the delivery of her second child. I had a difficult choice to make because my husband needed my help. I told her to please let me pray about it.

One day, I was preparing a meal in the kitchen and watching *One Night with the King*, a movie based on the book of Esther. Just like the biblical story, she fasted and prayed, asking the Lord to save her people from death. The Spirit of the Lord then spoke to me, *Fast about your daughter's request.* I asked her to give me three days. She called me back in two, so I did not yet have an answer for her but told her to speak with her father and ask him whether he could manage without me for a little while. He gave his consent for me to go to Hong Kong to assist with the delivery of her baby, and my eldest daughter, who lives with us, cared for her father.

In July 2014, I bought my ticket. My first stop was in the US. I visited with my son and left the next morning. On the day before my trip, my brother-in-law in Jamaica asked me if I would travel in my wheelchair. I told him no, but he suggested that it would be easier for me, so I took his advice. The next day, I was on my way. The plane landed in Shanghai before I boarded my final flight to Hong Kong. I found out that inclement weather conditions delayed my flight. I then realized the purpose of the wheelchair. The immigration officers did not pronounce my name properly, so my wheelchair assistant had to interpret their questions for me. I had to stay at the airport for the next day or two, but God favored me. My wheelchair assistant assured me that he would put me up in a hotel for the night and made sure I was comfortable on the bus ride over. I gave him a financial blessing as a gesture of gratitude. I relaxed and felt confident that He who had begun a good work would finish it.

Upon my arrival, I made myself comfortable, ate, and then got ready to sleep. I felt a bit anxious about oversleeping, as I had to rise early to ensure I did not miss the bus back to the airport. But all was well, and I was on time the next morning. While I waited at the hotel for the bus to arrive, my assistant asked me if I felt okay. In my mind, I was ready to catch the plane. I just wanted to be on my way. However, with a concerned look on his face, he said, "You are not alright. Have you eaten yet?" I responded no, and he directed me to the breakfast bar inside. He looked after my luggage while I ate.

The bus came for us shortly after. I was excited for the trip. The walk was short, so I did not need a wheelchair. With a sigh of relief, I boarded the plane. I found out later that my daughter had been tracking the aircraft, monitoring my every move! It was a good flight, and as I reached my destination, my family was ready to receive me. I gave God the glory for taking such good care of me. I later recalled the scripture that says, "Truly God is good to Israel, even to such as are of a clean heart" (Psalm 73:1).

> **I WAS OVERWHELMED BY WHAT GOD WAS DOING IN MY LIFE AS I PREPARED TO STEP OUT IN FAITH INTO THE UNKNOWN.**

I had only ever visited Hong Kong one other time. When I arrived, my family told me I could not go to sleep because of the different time zones. If I did, I would not be able to sleep later that night. So I tried to stay as productive as possible to keep myself awake. It was a different world there. The people were a little shorter than what I was accustomed to; even their homes were smaller than the homes in my country. On the day when I arrived, my daughter and her husband asked a friend to host her son and me. The host played one of Hillsong United's newest songs at the time, "Oceans (Where Feet May Fail)." The lyrics that ministered to me were, "Your sovereign hand will be my guide," and "Spirit, lead me where my trust is without borders."[2] For three months, my spirit man was very receptive to the song. I realized that the Spirit of the Lord wanted me to receive this song by faith because of where I was going spiritually. I was in need of active, uncompromising faith.

The next day, I arrived at my daughter's home, and the Holy Spirit asked me if I still wanted the surgery for my prolapsed bladder. I did. So, He asked me to pray to Him about it every day and anoint my body in expectation. So, I agreed to the challenge; almost every morning, I would play the Hillsong song and pray during the day. There were times when I did not know what to pray for. I would tell the Lord the truth from my heart, and He told me to give thanks. It made my journey with prayer a little easier. A faulty belief about prayer is that we should just pray once or twice about something and not bother God with the request again, but that signifies a great lack of faith. I began to realize that God led me to constantly come to Him about the matter and believe that He would respond to my request. Now I can appreciate the scripture "Pray without ceasing" (1 Thessalonians 5:17).

---

2 Hillsong United, vocalists, "Oceans (Where Feet May Fail)," by Joel Houston, Matt Crocker, and Salomon Lighthelm, released 2013, track 4 on *Zion*, Capitol CMG Publishing.

I spent three months with my daughter and her family in Hong Kong. As I reached the US, the doors for surgery opportunities began to open. One day, a friend of mine stopped by his pharmacy. I sat in the car with the radio on and heard the lyrics, "I am overwhelmed by you."[3] This song played over the airwaves all week. I was overwhelmed by what God was doing in my life as I prepared to step out in faith into the unknown.

## HIS DELIGHT TO PROVIDE

I was at my friend's home one Sunday night when in the early morning hours, I started to feel pain in my right leg. It was so strange; I had never felt anything like that before. Around 5:00 a.m., my friend and spiritual daughter took me to the emergency room. She is a registered nurse and helped me since I am not a citizen of that country. She was instructed to meet with the social worker and register me. I was put into the system and processed.

What would have taken a few weeks or a few months took me eleven days. I was mailed a medical card. My friend,

---

3 Big Daddy Weave, "Overwhelmed," by Johnny Redmond, released 2014, track 12 on *Love Come to Life,* Fervent Records.

her husband, and my husband in Jamaica were amazed. We all rejoiced and gave thanks for this move of God. They signed me up to see the gynecologist for testing. Secretly, in my heart, there were times when I was afraid because I did not know what would happen. But the Spirit of God reminded me that I needed to "In everything give thanks: for this is the will of God in Christ Jesus concerning you (1 Thessalonians 5:18). My medical journey took place in the height of winter—it was very cold, and I had to show up for every appointment, even if it was snowing. As the surgery drew closer, I became disheartened because I could not pay for a major test that cost USD$100. I had no funds. My social worker asked me if I could pay USD$50. I told her I could not.

Shortly after the social worker called, I learned that the full cost of this test was USD$3,000, so USD$100 was quite a discount. I asked the Holy Spirit whom I could ask to borrow USD$100. My brother from Chicago came into my spirit, so I made a call to him. He graciously agreed. After the last test, my surgery date was scheduled for mid-March of the following year. I was concerned about overstaying my welcome in the US, so I made plans to go back to Jamaica. At the church I was attending in the US, I met a prophet and explained my concern that returning home so soon would look suspicious, but he, too, believed it would be best.

## THE SPIRIT OF THE LORD GAVE ME DIVINE FAVOR THROUGHOUT THE WHOLE JOURNEY.

While I was undergoing the medical procedures, my son and daughter-in-law suggested that my granddaughter accompany me to Jamaica to visit for a while. That way, I could return to the US at a moment's notice for the surgery. So, I stayed in Jamaica with my granddaughter and then returned to the States a few weeks later. Immigration was satisfied with my response about the purpose of my trip home, which was to take my granddaughter back to her parents. I was relieved and very thankful that God had made the way for my return to do the surgery before it was even time for the surgery. The Spirit of the Lord gave me divine favor throughout the whole journey.

The night before my surgery, while staying with my spiritual daughter, I read about the surgery. I didn't see any information about the cost, and I worried about that. I did not know how it was going to be funded, and so I looked sad and worried when I arrived at the doctor's office. I inquired about payment, and the doctor just said, "Let's get the surgery over with, and then we can talk about the payment." Amazingly, it was never mentioned. All I can think is that the hospital social worker must have arranged to have everything covered. Thanks be to God!

It was a successful surgery, and I had no complications. I can testify that I remain well today. Can GOD do it? Yes, He can: "But without faith it is impossible to please him: for he that cometh to God must believe that He is, and that He is a rewarder of them that diligently seek him" (Hebrews 11:6).

# CHAPTER 7

# MY BIGGEST FEARS

I did not work between 1981 and 1983, so the Spirit spoke to me about doing a six-week refresher course in type-writing. After this, my husband asked me prophetically, "What if they call you to come back to work at your old job?" I thought about it for a few moments, then responded, "If that is what the Lord wants for me, I will accept." A few weeks later, my stepmother called and told me that she was going on leave for six weeks. She wanted me to come and work in her absence. Then I remembered the question my husband asked me about going back to my old job. I freely accepted and reported for work the following Monday. Although I was acquainted with exporting goods, she happily refreshed me on what else I needed to know.

When my time was up, I didn't know what my next move would be. Someone within the company asked me what I would do after I left my position as an export shipping clerk. They might have been fearful that I would take their position. I responded, "Maybe go back home."

## THEN, HE GRANTED ME HIS FAVOR YET AGAIN.

Suddenly the person said, "I know of a company that is hiring." And just like that, God opened doors again. She made a call. I was told to come in on Monday morning at 8:00 a.m. for an interview. I shared my fear of interviews with the Lord when I arrived and asked Him for success.

The factory manager arrived late, around 9:30 a.m. She apologized for being late, immediately introduced me to the staff, and told me what to do. I began working on the spot. She told me I could fill out the application later. I worked in this position for eight months—a good eight months, even in the face of warfare (many of my coworkers were threatened and feared I would take their position, so they did not welcome me.)

Then, He granted me His favor yet again. I was approached about another position and, this time, interviewed for it. It went well. I accepted their offer and started the new job as the assistant purchasing manager that same Monday. I worked there for eight and a half years. After resigning, I started my own business. Can GOD do it?

## DRIVING FEARS

When I started my own catering business, my husband encouraged me to get a driver's license to free up some of his time that he was spending to help me deliver lunches. He could not keep up with the demand of the business because of his teaching job. Think about the sacrifices he made—leave school, go home, drop off lunches, drop off the Mrs. at home, and return to work. It just was not going to work.

Studying for a driver's license test was successful, and I proudly received my driver's license and was ready to join the many commuters on the streets of Jamaica. Little did I know the two fears that would creep up:

1)  I drove a standard transmission car.
This meant I had to manually gear up and gear down my vehicle. Imagine driving fast and then being unable to slow down. In my mind, this was a dilemma; a crash was waiting to happen—this was trouble!

I had to go to the Lord in prayer about this. It was terrifying to experience on my first drive and, even worse, think about what day two would bring. That night, after praying, the Lord took my hand in a dream and showed me how to gear down with the shift stick. It was a tangible and powerful experience! I woke up with confidence, knowing that this would no longer be an issue, but what came next was certainly a test I had to pass.

2) A foul spirit came to me in the hallway.

I cooked, shared, boxed, and packed all the lunches for delivery. It was time to go . . . then it happened. I felt backed against the wall. A demon taunted me that I had no way of leaving the house because the reverse gear was part of the gear-down position. I shook with fear. How was I going to leave? The tormenting voice kept jeering. A boldness came upon me, and I told this devil to take the keys out of my hand and drive the car out. I waited for a minute, and nothing happened. I said, "Please excuse me!" With the keys in my hand, I got in the car, started the ignition, backed out, and drove with no problems. I could change gears easily.

Can GOD do it?

## ALL THANKS TO GOD

I really want to thank God for His blessings. The Word of God declares, "The blessing of the Lord, it maketh rich, and he addeth no sorrow with it" (Proverbs 10:22). We were able to acquire a Toyota HiAce van to go to the country to sell goods. There, we saw tremendous growth in the business. So, we had four vehicles, and the Lord told us to bless the church with one of the vehicles for missionary work. I remember the Lord blessed us, and the devil came to me and said, "You can brag and boast about what you have acquired now." My response was, "How do you do that?" and I had to rebuke him. I didn't know what it was like to "brag" or "boast." That was not in my spirit; my spirit was in a place where I humbly thanked God for His graciousness in helping me and my family turn our lives around in such a profound way.

# CHAPTER 8

# GETTING TO KNOW THE HOLY SPIRIT

In 2016, I came back to Jamaica only partially recovered. I had just undergone major surgery myself in the US. My husband had promised my family and friends that he would make sure I got the necessary rest I needed to recover, but that never happened. Within a few weeks of our return, my husband suffered a major stroke at the base of his brain stem. This happened only two days after our eldest, the praying newborn, dreamt of her father vomiting blood on a Wednesday afternoon. The stroke happened on Friday. My back gave way over the weekend, but I had to care for my husband. I found myself gravely weakened from surgery, unable to lift anything heavy or push my body beyond reasonable limits. Because I had to assist him constantly, my back continued to act up. I was in so much pain that morning. Nevertheless, I had to make every effort to attend to my husband. I had to lift and turn my husband in the bed. This was no easy task—turning him meant bracing his body with my own, putting the weight of his body upon mine—for the love of all my body and soul.

Nurses were assigned to care for my husband, but when they had days off, I was his primary caregiver. Each day, I had to make his breakfast until the morning nurse arrived, which meant literally crawling out of bed, slowly straightening my back, and walking into the kitchen to make his breakfast. I was becoming a little weary of taking care of my husband and handling all the needs that come with caring for a person who has suffered a major stroke.

I did my best to quickly return to bed to stretch out because the discomfort was unbearable. As I was lying down, I remembered I had clothes in the washing machine that needed hanging on the line. Due to the severe pain, I could not manage to crawl out of bed again, so I called for the nurse in the other room. There was no response for some time—I thought she may have been on the phone. Just then, I heard the Holy Spirit whisper to me, "Would you like me to call her for you?" I was taken aback and wondered if I had heard correctly (though, of course, I knew Holy Spirit's voice). I smiled and said yes. In less than a minute, the nurse came to my door and asked me if I had called her. I laughed and told her that I couldn't get her attention and so the Holy Spirit offered to do it for me. I requested her assistance with the laundry. Matthew 7:7 says, "Ask, and it shall be given to you; seek, and ye shall find; knock, and it shall be opened unto you." I have had numerous encounters with the Holy Spirit's help. If at any time I needed to find anything that had been misplaced, He would help me when I asked for it— for healing, financial help, or any other difficult situations. Indeed, He is "our refuge and strength," and He, the spirit of truth, is "a very present help in trouble" (Psalm 46:1).

More and more, I find the presence of the Holy Spirit, the Comforter, to be my safe haven.

With God's help, I quickly adjusted. The Spirit of the Lord spoke to my spirit about a shape I had previously seen made by the grounds at the bottom of my coffee cup. The grounds had settled in the shape of a heart. He said, *Take care of my servant.* My husband was the Bishop Emeritus of our church organization. Moving on a few months later, the heart appeared once again. Its appearance still surprised me. Perhaps I had forgotten about what I had seen before, but I knew it was important for me to pay attention to the assignment I was given to love my husband. It is important to serve from a good place and with the right spirit, though I did not know I would lose my husband. He was taken to his heavenly home. So, it was and is very important to "Keep thy heart with all diligence; for out of it are the issues of life" (Proverbs 4:23)

and "And whatsoever ye do in word or deed, do all in the name of the Lord Jesus, giving thanks to God and the Father by him" (Colossians 3:17).

## WHEN GOD GETS PERSONAL

My personal experience with the Holy Spirit started when I was about twenty-four years old. At that time, I became aware of the Holy Spirit's involvement in my life, and I began paying much more attention. He would speak to me through His Word, silently in my spirit. This began in my early adult life, but I didn't fully understand, nor was I mature enough to notice that He wanted to build a closer relationship with me. Before and after marriage, I devoted myself to prayer and the Word. One morning long ago, He said to me, *There is something in your spirit; take it up and look at it.*

> HE DESIRES INTIMACY WITH US AND WANTS TO REVEAL THINGS TO THOSE WHO SEEK HIM.

As the days, months, and years passed, whenever I shared and encouraged others, I would often say to them, as they shared their concerns with me, "There is something in your spirit. All you need to do is stop, take it up, and look at it." They were surprised to find that the Holy Spirit had deposited something in their spirits and were able to identify what the Spirit of God was speaking to them. He brings a word, a song, and guidance to show His love and care for His children. He desires intimacy with us and wants to reveal things to those who seek Him.

I would search for the song or word He gave me, and He would alert me to trials or upcoming events. He would also guide me on when to fast or provide insight into any medical issues. He rebuked or corrected me when necessary, and I've had to ask for His forgiveness several times. I've learned to rely on Him in every aspect of my life, trusting that He knows the deep things of God and helps me in my weaknesses.

When I would ask Him to wake me up if a family member was out, especially at night, He honored my request or brought them to my thoughts. He even asked me if I needed specific amounts of money, and when I confirmed it was His voice, He provided. He guided my grocery lists and provided funds for them. Whenever I misplaced something, I would ask Him to help me locate it, and I would find it.

On one memorable occasion, my grandson lost his school bag, and after praying, we found it weeks later under the sofa. I believe that as a grandmother, it is important to help acquaint the next generation with God's Spirit and His Word. I've had numerous encounters with the Holy Spirit's help in healing, financial matters, and difficult situations. He truly is a present help in times of trouble.

**MY ENCOUNTER WITH THE HOLY SPIRIT HAS DEEPENED MY LOVE FOR HIM, AND I'M GRATEFUL FOR HIS CONSTANT PRESENCE IN MY LIFE.**

I could list many more instances of His guidance and provision, such as directing me to attend fasting services or showing me where to start a business. He's spoken to me about my children, their walk with Him, healing, traveling, ministry, and even restoring my love life. I've learned to acknowledge God in all my ways, and He directs my path.

My encounter with the Holy Spirit has deepened my love for Him, and I'm grateful for His constant presence in my life. Despite my imperfections, His grace sustains me, and I'm reminded of Romans 8:28, "And we know that all things work together for good to them that love God, to them who are the called according to *his* purpose." These experiences are meant to conform me to the image of His Son, Jesus.

On Christmas Eve of 2015, God miraculously provided the exact amount I needed to pay for my husband's care through unexpected means. It was a reminder of His promise in Psalm 46:1: "God is our refuge and strength, a very present help in trouble."

In 2016, during a difficult time with my husband's illness, I experienced the Holy Spirit's intervention when my back gave out. Despite the pain, He provided help when I needed it, showing me His faithfulness in caring for His children. I prayed for our two vehicles to sell, and God sent a buyer who not only purchased the vehicles but also provided unexpected financial assistance. It was a testimony to God's faithfulness and provision.

In prayer one evening, the Holy Spirit asked me if I would be the pastor of the assembly where I had previously attended. I was off the island for a while, so I did not think that the Lord, by His Spirit, would have called me to pastor at this time of my life. In a prayer meeting held at my home, I cried and cried as I felt the conviction of the Spirit of God. This was unexpected but confirmed previous messages from God about my role in ministry. The truth is that in 1991, awaking from my sleep, the Lord, by His Spirit, had said to me, *Write this: Your daughter and yourself will be pastors.* I immediately got my diary and pen from my bedside table and wrote what was said to me by the Spirit of God. My eldest daughter had a similar experience. In her deep sleep, the Lord also spoke to her. And once, in her devotional time, He spoke to her again, saying, *Feed my sheep.*

Despite my initial hesitation, I obeyed. I was ordained in 2019, and during my two-year tenure, God blessed the church with growth and financial provision.

Looking ahead, I am excited to share upcoming resources and continue proclaiming the goodness of God's faithfulness and provision in my life. Can GOD do it? Yes, He can do anything!

# ABOUT THE AUTHOR

Viviene A. Kitson, a distinguished figure in the realm of spiritual leadership, hails from Kingston, Jamaica, where she has gracefully navigated life's journey for 71 years. With a marriage that spanned 42 years until her beloved husband, Bishop Derrick Kitson, departed for his heavenly abode in 2017, Viviene's life has been a testament to unwavering faith and dedication.

Her spiritual odyssey began at the tender age of 15 when she embraced Jesus into her heart, setting the foundation for a lifetime of impactful ministry. For over four decades, Viviene has been an integral part of the House of Prayer and

Praise Ministries, assuming pivotal roles such as Evangelism Director and Women's President, illuminating pathways of hope and transformation.

In 2006, Viviene's commitment to theological excellence was underscored as she obtained a Diploma in Practical Theology from the esteemed International Seminary in Plymouth, Florida. This academic milestone further fortified her capacity to lead, teach, and inspire others on their spiritual journeys.

Her legacy extends beyond the realms of ministry, as Viviene has also excelled in the realm of entrepreneurship as a professional caterer and businesswoman. Amidst her multifaceted roles, she finds joy in hobbies such as cooking, indulging in literary treasures, nurturing her backyard garden, and embarking on enriching travel adventures.

Viviene currently holds the esteemed roles of a nurturing mother to two young men and two young women, and a cherished grandmother to ten adoring grandchildren. Alongside her familial responsibilities, she serves as a dedicated

Pastor, offering her ministerial services as needed within the divine realms. Her overarching mission is to catalyze transformative experiences by guiding individuals towards a profound, personal connection with Jesus Christ while nurturing a deep intimacy with the Holy Spirit.

Driven by a global vision, Viviene aspires to extend her impactful reach to men and women worldwide, traversing borders and cultures in her quest to bring spiritual enlightenment and empowerment.

Among her many accolades, Viviene stands proudly as a beacon of support and inspiration within the Jamaica Association of Full Gospel Churches, where her exceptional contributions have garnered special recognition. With an impressive tenure of 42 years in active ministry and two years of dedicated pastoral leadership, Viviene Kitson exemplifies unwavering dedication, profound wisdom, and a boundless commitment to uplifting and transforming lives within the kingdom of God.

# CAN GOD DO IT?

# YES, HE CAN!

www.ingramcontent.com/pod-product-compliance
Lightning Source LLC
Chambersburg PA
CBHW051432090426
42737CB00014B/2934